AN ATLAS OF ANCIENT EGYPT.

WITH COMPLETE INDEX,
GEOGRAPHICAL AND HISTORICAL NOTES,
BIBLICAL REFERENCES, ETC.

by Egypt Exploration Fund

ISBN: 978-1-63923-603-9

Printed: January 2023

Published and Distributed By:
Lushena Books
607 Country Club Drive, Unit E
Bensenville, IL 60106
www.lushenabks.com

ISBN: 978-1-63923-603-9

CONTENTS.

PREFACE.

THE Committee of the Egypt Exploration Fund issues this volume of Maps of Ancient Egypt as a Special Publication, in the belief that many of its friends and subscribers may desire to possess such an Atlas exhibiting the latest identifications of ancient sites, and more especially marking the important geographical discoveries which have resulted from the work of the Society.

Egypt changes but little, and the modern Map, with the natural as well as the artificial features depicted upon it, will give a truer insight into the physiography of the country in ancient times than the skeleton maps of Ancient Egypt which follow it. This map also shows the lines of the modern desert roads (which generally coincide with those of the old roadways), the Egyptian railway system, and the Suez Canal; it will therefore be appreciated by travellers, as well as by archæological enquirers. Opposite to the maps of Ancient Egypt will be found tables containing the names of the Nomes and their capitals, and of the local gods, but the state of our present knowledge does not enable us to delineate their boundaries; which, moreover, often varied.

Maps of the Wady Tumîlât and the Land of Goshen have already been published by the Egypt Exploration Fund as part of the results of M. Naville's researches conducted for the Society, and explained at length in his Memoirs of 1884 and 1887. The present Map of that district is compiled from them, and extracts from the Memoirs which bear upon the maps are also reprinted. A reference list of localities in Egypt mentioned in the Bible is appended for the use of Bible students.

Since this Atlas will doubtless fall into the hands of many who have had neither time nor opportunity for the study of Egyptology, interested as they may be in its results, a few notes on certain geographical aspects of Ancient Egyptian history are here given.

INTRODUCTION.

THE ANCIENT EGYPTIANS AND THEIR COUNTRY; THEIR FOREIGN INTERCOURSE.

The Egyptian population, its origin and character.— The land of Egypt, stretching from the Mediterranean to Aswân on the Nubian frontier, has an area of only 10,292 square miles, with a present population of nearly 7 millions, or about 600 people to the square mile. In extent the country has remained unaltered from remotest historic times, but its ancient population is supposed to have been more dense than that of to-day ; in the age of Josephus (A.D. 37—100) it appears to have numbered at least 7½ millions. Some authorities hold that the Ancient Egyptians were of African origin, and from the South. Others maintain that they came from the North-East by the isthmus of Suez; or from the East by Kûs and Coptos; or from the South-East by the straits of Bab el Mandeb; their original home, according to these several opinions, having been in Asia Minor, in Central Asia, or in South Arabia. But, whatever their origin, this at least is clear to us—from the earliest times of which any historic record survives, the strong, mystic, and subtle individuality of the people was fully marked and developed; and the physical characteristics of their country are so correspondingly distinctive that it is difficult not to consider these as the main cause of that distinction in life, religion, and art which is so much a thing apart that we can only describe it as Ancient Egyptian.

Egypt "the gift of the Nile." The Delta and its changes.—Egypt is little more than the bed of the Nile. Her fertile Delta was formed by the accumulation of alluvial deposits at the mouth of the river during pre-historic times, and was so called by the Greeks on account of the resemblance of its outline to that of the fourth letter of their alphabet. In the maps of this Atlas the courses of the river and canals, and the outlines of lakes are represented as those of the present day, since it is impossible to restore the ancient beds with certainty. The Greek historians and geographers tell us that the Nile divided into three main branches at the southern point of the Delta, and that these subdivided, so that the river entered the sea by seven channels, of which five were natural, and two artificial. But these have all more or less changed, dwindled, or disappeared. In order from East to West, they were named by the Greeks—the Pelusiac, Tanitic, Mendesian, Phatnitic, Sebennytic, Bolbitine, and Canopic branches, generally after the principal cities through which they passed. In the days of Herodotus, the fork of the river was three or four miles north of where Cairo stands; it is now some ten miles further north still. The Rosetta and Damietta branches of the Nile are its two chief outlets at the present day, and they may be taken as roughly corresponding with the Canopic and Phatnitic channels. The Pelusiac branch has disappeared. The elusive character of the internal geography of Ancient Egypt largely results from natural variations in the distribution of the waters of the river; from great artificial changes of the water-system (notably those made in the times of Mena, the first historic king; of the XIIth and XIXth Dynasties; and of the Ptolemies); and, lastly, from the cumulative effects of local irrigation continued for thousands of years.

Lower and Upper Egypt, Nubia, and the Faiyum.— To the Egyptians, the Delta was "the Land of the North" (or Lower Egypt). The rest of their country was "the Land of the South" (or Upper Egypt), and extended from the apex of the Delta to the ridge of granite which crosses the Nile at about 24'' N. latitude and produces the "first cataract." This cataract marked the confines of the Land of Nubia (the Ethiopia of Greek and Roman geographers), known to the Egyptians as the Land of Kash, and one of their earliest conquests. Upper Egypt (including the Faiyûm) has an average width of only 10 miles, with a length of about 450; and this also is "the gift of the Nile."[1] It is hemmed in by the hills of the Arabian and Libyan deserts, and its rich black soil is entirely formed of the deposit left by the annual overflowing of the river. The Faiyûm is a natural depression surrounded by the Libyan hills, 840 square miles in area, and about 50 miles south-

[1] *Herodotus* II, 5.

west of Cairo. The Bahr Yûsif, a water-course diverging from the river near Asyût, enters the Faiyûm through the gorge of El Lahûn, and thus connects the province with the valley of the Nile. The Faiyûm was anciently renowned for its fertility, and is still well cultivated; its name is derived from an Egyptian word signifying "marsh, or lake district," through its Coptic form of *Phiôm*. Here was the celebrated "Lake Moeris" of the Greeks, the admiration of Herodotus and the work of the xiith Dynasty kings; who also built the adjoining "Labyrinth," and were buried near to it, within the pyramids of Hawâreh and El Lahûn. These kings turned the natural lake, formed by drainage and the annual overflow of the Nile, into the artificially controlled reservoir of Lake Moeris. At its highest, the original lake of the Faiyûm had almost covered the province; as reduced, it seems to have had a perimeter of 136 miles, and a greatest depth of 230 feet.[2] To the ancient inhabitants their river was *Hapi*, and their country *Kemt*, the Black Land; while the sandy desert was *Teshert*, the Red Land. The Greeks called the country *Aiguptos*, and its river *Neilos*, whence, through the Latin forms of *Ægyptus* and *Nilus*, come our names of Egypt and the Nile. Little or no rain falls in Upper Egypt, although the climate is said to be now changing in this respect. The necessary irrigation of the crops has always depended upon the due storing and distribution of the waters of the yearly inundation.

Ancient Quarries.—Owing to the scarcity of wood, Egyptian buildings were generally made of bricks of Nile-mud: monumental works were constructed of hard or fine-grained stones, which were abundantly found in the rocky edges of the Nile valley. The rock on both sides of the river, and as far as Silsileh, is limestone of various qualities, and there is hardly half a mile of cliff without quarries; perhaps the finest quality was obtained opposite Memphis at Turah. A patch of hard quartzite is found close to Cairo at Gebel Aḥmar, and numerous fine monuments in this material exist. Alabaster was quarried especially in the *Het Nub* region on the east bank from Mi nyehto Asyût. In the southern portion of Upper Egypt, sandstone took the place of limestone as the chief

[2] See *The Fayûm and Lake Moeris*, by Major R. H. Brown, R.E., Inspector General of Irrigation, Upper Egypt; 1892.

material for stone construction, and the most notable quarry is at
Gebel Silsileh, where the rocks on either side approach and over-
hang the river, so that the removal of the blocks was easily effected.
Red granite and some grey granite were quarried at Syene, the
cataract there being formed by a vein of this *syenite*[1] crossing
the river valley.   Between the Nile and the Red Sea was a great
variety of fine materials, such as basalt, granite, diorite, porphyry ;
the latter, perhaps, worked only by the Romans.   The difficulties
of obtaining them did not deter even the earliest kings of the ivth
Dynasty from making the freest use of these stones for their
"monuments of eternity."

**Egyptian mythology; its connection with the geography
of Egypt.**—The true sources of their beneficent Nile, and the
causes of its regular rise and fall in the summer and autumn months
were as unknown to the Ancient Egyptians as the origin of the great
Sun himself.   His nightly disappearance behind the Western, or
Libyan hills suggested to them that land of darkness to which their
dead passed on, and hence they preferred to found their cemeteries,
or cities of the dead, on the west bank of the river.   In early
times, travellers' tales of the oases of the Libyan waste doubtless
led to the belief that beyond the perils of the desert, and beyond
a fearful country which the dead must traverse, if they did not
perish by the way, the islands of the blest were to be found.   The
Ancient Egyptians deified all natural phenomena which they recognised as regular and persistent, and chief among their beneficent
deities were different forms of the Sun-god, and also Osiris, the
fertilizing power of the river.   The barren desert, ever ready to
encroach upon their tilled and fertile fields, was inimical to life
in the eyes of a settled and agricultural people such as they were.[2]
The desert was therefore personified in the destructive god Set;
and between Set and Osiris had been constant rivalry and warfare
corresponding to the unending encroachments of desert on fertile
land, and fertile land on desert.

**The State Religion and the Government; their feudal
character.**—The gods of the Ancient Egyptians were essentially

---

[1] This is, however, not the true Syenite of mineralogists.

[2] Incidental reference is made to this fact in *Genesis* xlvii, 31—34.   The "shepherds" here
referred to were nomads of the Eastern desert, who were always troublesome to the Egyptians.

local gods—gods of a district, or even of a city. Their chief deities represented the Sun, the Earth, the principal planets and stars, and the Nile; all these being worshipped under different aspects, and considered both as gods of the living and of the dead. The essential unity of their natures made it easy for any one of the local gods to be regarded as national, if his city became the chief seat of government and the home of the reigning dynasty. The kings were supposed to be of divine descent, and were, theoretically, the great high priests of their dominions; so that, notwithstanding the number and variety of their local deities, the Egyptians still had a national religion. The system of government can best be described as feudal; it was bound up with the state religion, and its administration was based upon the subdivision of the land.

The Nomes and their Princes.—Upper and Lower Egypt were divided into some forty provinces, the number and boundaries of which might vary from time to time. These provinces were called *hesep* by the natives, and by the Greeks *nomoi*; whence the modern term Nomes. Each nome had its farm-land; its marshes for fowling and the cultivation of papyrus reeds; its canal; and its capital, which was the centre of the provincial religion and administration. Great vassal princes were the hereditary rulers of the nomes and high priests of the local temples, being responsible to the king for the due maintenance of civil crder, and military efficiency. Their duties consisted in loyalty to the person and interests of the king, in levying, etc., in care for the well-being of their vassals, and in the military discipline and command of all their able-bodied men.[1]

Communication with foreign nations.—Sometimes the king sent his nobles on exploring and aggressive expeditions, whence they were expected to return with treasure which it might please them to call the gifts or tribute of other lands. Such expeditions brought back fine material for the use of the sculptor, precious metals, stones, woods, and incense, costly articles of foreign workmanship, natural curiosities and products, and added to the variety of

---

[1] See the biographical inscriptions of *Beni Hasan I*" and "*Beni Hasan II*," for particulars as to the conduct of exemplary nomarchs.

the indigenous flora and fauna of Egypt, which is naturally but limited.   Hostile, commercial, and general national intercourse was thus gradually established with Nubia and the Sûdân, the Libyan and other North African peoples, desert tribes, the inhabitants of the Sinaitic peninsula, Syria, Babylonia, and Mesopotamia, the traders and dwellers on the coasts of the Red Sea and in Arabia, the kingdoms of Asia Minor, the Phœnicians, and the pre-Homeric Greeks.   In the seventh century B.C. Greek colonists (traders and mercenary troops) were formally recognised by the Egyptians.

The invasions of Egypt by foreign nations.—Egypt was conquered by the Hyksôs[2] not much later than 2000 B.C.; by the Ethiopians under Sabako B.C. 700; by the Assyrians under Esarhaddon and Assurbanipal B.C. 672—665; by the Persians under Cambyses B.C. 525; and fell, as part of the empire of Persia, into the hands of Alexander B.C. 333.   But it is only from the Hebrews, and from Greeks, by birth or culture, that we have any foreign accounts of her civilisation before it was merged in that of the Roman Empire.   The Greeks linked the life of Ancient Egypt with that of Europe; and it is primarily to Greek accounts that we owe our first knowledge of this country of their conquest and adoption.

[2] The Hyksôs have not yet been identified.   They are stated by Josephus to have been "Shepherd Kings," and to have come from the North East.

SUMMARY

OF

M. NAVILLE'S GEOGRAPHICAL DISCOVERIES
RELATING TO THE SOJOURN OF THE ISRAELITES IN EGYPT,
AND TO
THE ROUTE OF THE EXODUS.

In the first and fourth "Memoirs" of the Egypt Exploration Fund,
M. Naville has endeavoured to trace the route of the Exodus;
his conclusions are drawn from the results of his excavations
and researches at Saft-el-Henneh studied in the light of ancient
historical and geographical records. These conclusions, with the
arguments that led to them, are here summarised, and followed
by an extensive quotation of the chapter on the "Route of the
Exodus" from his Memoir entitled *The Store City of Pithom.*[1]

Up to 1883, the mound of Tell el Maskhutah was supposed by
Egyptologists to occupy the site of the city of Raamses (*Exodus* I,
11); in the spring of that year M. Naville found it to be on that
of Pithom.

By the' study of the inscriptions on monuments which had already
been taken from the place and were then in Ismailiah, and of those
which he himself discovered among the ruins, M. Naville found that
the god of the city had been Tum, that its religious name had been
Pi-Tum—the Abode of Tum, and that the temple had been situate
in the civil city of Thukut. The name Pi-Tum corresponds with
the Hebrew *Pithom*, the Coptic *Pethom*, and the *Peitho*
of the Septuagint. The founder of the place appeared to be
Rameses II (XIXth Dynasty, B.C. 1300—1250),[2] who is usually
supposed to be the Pharaoh of the Oppression, and it had evidently
been built as a fortified military store-house or granary (*Exodus* I,
11; the Hebrew word here means *store-houses*, the Septuagint

---

[1] The third and revised edition of M. Naville's *Store City of Pithom and the Route of the
Exodus* was published in 1887, after the discovery and excavation of Goshen, and the friendly
criticism of the First Edition by Biblical critics and Egyptologists all the world over.

[2] The dates of Ancient Egyptian history, in round numbers, as given throughout this letter-
press are, as far as possible, in accordance with those to which Professor Flinders Petrie has
recently given currency in his lectures delivered at University College, London.

translates *fortified cities*), in which provisions were gathered for the use of armies or caravans bound across the Eastern desert. The bricks of which these "military store-houses" were built were composed of the common material, Nile mud, mixed with chopped straw; but in places they were apparently made without straw (*Exodus* v, 6—19).

The name Thuku occurs repeatedly in those letters of scribes and officials of the XIXth Dynasty which constitute the so-called Anastasi papyri, and is there followed by the determinative (a hieroglyphic symbol, marking the nature of the preceding word), indicating a borderland inhabited by foreigners. In these writings the name denotes a district including "the lakes of Pithom of Menephthes, which is of Thuku," and it is hence clear that before becoming the civil name of the capital, Thuku designated a region, or district, containing Pithom. Such was the meaning of the name under the XIXth Dynasty. M. Naville also gives his philological reasons for considering Succoth (*Exodus* XII, 37; XIII, 20) as the Hebrew equivalent of Thuku.[8]

Among the Roman ruins of the mound M. Naville further discovered two inscribed stones, one bearing the words ERO CASTRA, the camp of Ero; and the second reading as follows:—

> *Dominis nostris victoribus, Maximiano et Severo imperatoribus, et Maximino et Constantino nobilissimis Caesaribus, ab Ero in Clusma, M. VIIII—θ.*

> *Under our victorious lords, the emperors Maximianus and Severus, and the most illustrious Caesars Maximinus and Constantine, from Ero to Clusma there are nine miles—Nine.*

As was usual in the Roman provinces where Greek was spoken, the distance is given both in Latin and Greek, and the θ at the end of the last line stands for nine. This Roman milestone was the means of leading M. Naville to the conclusion that Pi-Tum was the Heroöpolis of the Greeks. In the English Bible (*Genesis* XLVI, 28), we read that Jacob, going to Egypt, "sent Judah before him unto Joseph, to direct his face unto Goshen." Here the Septuagint, whose writers must have known the geography of Egypt, translates instead of "unto Goshen," unto "Heroöpolis in the land of Ramses." The Memphite Coptic version, which was translated from the

---

[8] It must here be said that Brugsch's philological argument for the identification of Thukut and Succoth is not admitted by M. Maspero.

Septuagint, keeps the old name of the city, and has "near Pethom, the city in the land of Ramses"; showing that at the time when this version was made, in the fourth century A.D., Heroöpolis was still for the natives the abode of the God "TUM," who possibly was not yet dethroned by Christianity. In Egyptian, *Ar* or *Era*, when followed by the hieroglyphic sign denoting a building, means a store-house, and the first part of the Greek name for this store city may be the Greek transliteration of the Egyptian word "*Era*." The Greek and Roman writers who speak of Heroöpolis are unanimous in declaring that the city was near the sea, at the head of the Arabian Gulf, which was also called Heroöpolitan, and hence it is assumed that even in the times of the Romans the Red Sea extended much further north than it does now, and that the Bitter Lakes were then under water. Linant Bey considered it geologically proved that, under the Pharaohs of the XIXth Dynasty, Lake Timsah and the valleys of Saba Biar and Abu Balah were part of the Red Sea. This view is confirmed by the physical features of the country, for the depression of Lake Timsah has a narrow extension towards the west, presenting the appearance of the head of a gulf. The sea would thus have extended to within three miles of Heroöpolis. Gradually the water withdrew, communication between city and gulf was partly cut off, and where the Red Sea had been there remained only salt marshes, which were called by Strabo and Pliny the *Bitter Lakes*.[1]

M. Naville also found at Tell el Maskhutah an historical tablet of Ptolemy Philadelphos in whose reign (B.C. 286—247) the Septuagint version of the Hebrew Scriptures was begun in Alexandria. This tablet gives many data which not only confirm the discoveries already mentioned, but also show that another great temple of the VIIIth Nome was Pikerehet, dedicated to Osiris. Pikerehet plays an important part in the tablet, the last lines of which give the amount of taxes which were granted as income to

---

[1] Professor Sayce (in *The Higher Criticism and the Monuments*, S.P.C.K. 1894; pp. 259—60) specially emphasises the objections to M. Naville's theory of the Route of the Exodus. Up to the present time, none of the various theories can claim sufficient proof to warrant an exclusive acceptance, and until further and careful examinations of the character, date and situation of ancient remains between Lake Timsah and the Gulf of Suez have been made, no satisfactory explanation of the Biblical statements is to be expected.

that temple. In the different Nome lists it is also named, alter-
natively with Pi-Tum, as the chief sanctuary of the VIIIth Nome
of Lower Egypt, and always as belonging to the region of Thuku.
M. Naville therefore concludes that this region contained two important sanctuaries very near to each other, Pi-Tum and Pikerehet,
the latter being the closer to the sea. The Greeks called a temple
of Osiris a Serapeum, and the official itinerary of the Roman Empire
mentions a city of Serapeum, or Serapiu, as being some eighteen
miles distant from Ero; and since we know of no other temple of
Osiris in the neighbourhood of Heroöpolis, Pikerehet must be the
Serapiu of the Itinerary. There are no traces of ruins which can
be the remains of Pikerehet—Serapiu, excepting those at the foot
of Gebel Mariam.

The tablet speaks of the horses and cattle given to the
sanctuary of Pikerehet for its annual support. A passage
from one of the XIXth Dynasty Anastasi papyri already mentioned, indicates that the more immediate eastern neighbourhood of Pi-Tum was known as the estate or farm of Pharaoh.
Now the "before Pi-hahiroth" of *Exodus* XIV, 2, is translated in the
Septuagint and the Coptic versions as "before the farm." Hence
M. Naville concludes that the Pi-hahiroth of the Hebrews was the
Pikerehet of the Nome lists, and of the tablet of Ptolemy Philadelphos.

GOSHEN.

M. NAVILLE's researches at Saft-el-Henneh led him to identify it
as the site of Pi Sopt (the *Abode of Sopt*), which was the religious
capital of the XXth Nome of Lower Egypt. This Nome was
known to the Egyptians as the Nome of Sopt or Soptakhem, and
Professor Brugsch discovered that it was identical with the Arabian
Nome of Greek and Roman writers. The civil capital of the
Nome was Pa Kes, from which came its Greek name of Phacusa
(*Pha-Cusa*). M. Naville found this name "*Kes*" in the inscriptions
of the shrine of Nectanebo II (XXXth Dynasty, B.C. 367—350),
at Saft-el-Henneh, and in such connections as showed that it

was at the civil capital called "Kes," that Nectanebo erected this shrine, in the religious capital, "Pi Sopt." Therefore Phacusa ("Pa Kes"), the secular capital, and Pi Sopt or Pa Sopt, the religious capital of the xxth Nome, both stood upon the site now occupied by the modern village of Saft-el-Henneh. The names of Goshen and Phacusa have the same origin in ancient Egyptian.[1] In the Septuagint the land of Goshen is called *Gesem of Arabia*, i.e., *Gesem, which is in the Nome of Arabia*, and the term, though strictly referring to a limited district, may yet have applied to the whole country occupied by the Israelites. Kesem (Gesem) is mentioned in such connections, and with such hieroglyphic determinatives in the Temple lists of offerings from the various districts, as to show that it is the civil name of the district and city in which stood the Temple of Sopt, the God of the Arabian Nome, and hence the land of Goshen was the country around Saft-el-Henneh, within the triangle lying between the villages of Saft, Belbeis and Tel-el-Kebir. Again, the Coptic translation of *Genesis* xlv, 10, gives for our Goshen—Kesem of T—arabia; and T—arabia, "the Arabia," in Coptic corresponds to what the Arabs call the Hauf, i.e., the land between the Nile and the Red Sea, which constitutes the present province of Sharkieh, and where the Nome of Arabia was situate. M. Naville further concludes that at the time when the Israelites occupied the land, the name "Goshen" belonged to a region which had as yet no definite boundaries, and which extended with the increase of the people over the territory they inhabited. He also thinks that the term "land of Ramses" (*Genesis* xlvii, 11) applied to a larger area, and included that part of the Delta which lies to the eastward of the Tanitic branch, a country which Rameses ii (xixth Dynasty, B.C. 1300—1250) enriched with innumerable works of architecture, and which corresponds with the present province of Sharkieh. The *city* of Raamses (*Exodus* i, 11) was situate in the Arabian Nome, but its identification cannot be regarded as established.

---

1 In the Proceedings of the Society of Biblical Archæology for June 1893, and writing on the newly ascertained Egyptian personification and worship of the zodiacal lights of the morning and evening twilights—the God Sopt being that divine personification, and Pi Sopt or Pa Sopt the chief seat of his worship—Brugsch shows that Gesem, the Coptic form of the ancient Egyptian name Keset, which was the name of the civil city Phacusa, means "the city of the twilights." The land of Goshen was so called as belonging to the city of Goshen.

THE ROUTE OF THE EXODUS.[*]

Among the historical events upon which the discovery of Pithom tends to throw light, one of the most important is certainly the Exodus, and the route which the Israelites followed in going out of Egypt. The Israelites were settled in the land of Goshen, in a region which perhaps extended further northward, but which certainly comprehended the Wady Tumilât, wherein was situated the city of Pithom, where, according to the Septuagint, Jacob and Joseph met when the Patriarch came to Egypt. Bound for Palestine, two different routes lay before them. The northern route had been followed by the great conquerors. It went from Tanis to the Syrian coast; it was the shortest way, but it went through several fortresses, particularly the great stronghold of *Zar*. Besides, the first part of it crossed a well-cultivated and irrigated land occupied by an agricultural population, which was not a land of pasture necessary for a people of shepherds. This northern route is called in the Bible, *the way of the land of the Philistines;* and, from the first, before any other indication as to the direction they followed, it is said that the Israelites did not take that road. The other was the southern route, which their ancestor Jacob had taken before them, and which, according to Linant Bey, was still followed by the Bedawin of our days before the opening of the canal. They went straight from El Arish to the valley of Saba Biar; while the traders, travelling through Kantarah, Salihieh, and Korein, followed very nearly the old northern route. The Israelites had only to go along the canal as far as its opening into the Arabian Gulf at a short distance from Succoth ; then, pushing straight forward, they would skirt the northern shore of the Gulf, and reach the desert and the Palestine way without having any sea to cross.

"The children of Israel journeyed from Rameses to Succoth." It is useless now to discuss the site of the city of Rameses, which will only be ascertained by further excavations. It is quite possible that we must here understand the name as referring to the *land* of Rameses rather than to the *city* ; the land must have been either west or north of Pithom. The first station is *Succoth, Thukut*, or *Thuku*. Here it is important to observe that the name of the

* From Prof. Naville's *Pithom*, 3rd edition, pp. 27—31.

place where the Israelites first encamped is not the name of a city but the name of a district, of the region of Thukut, in which, at the time of the Exodus, there existed not only Pithom, but the fortifications which Rameses II, his predecessor, and successor had erected to keep off the plundering tribes of Bedawin. It is quite natural that the camping ground of such a large multitude must have had a great extent. It was not at Pithom that the Israelites halted; the gates of the fortified city were not opened to them, nor were the store-houses. Besides, the area of the enclosure would have been quite insufficient to contain such a vast crowd. They pitched their tents in the land of Succoth where Pithom was built, very likely near those lakes and those good pastures to which the nomads of Atuma asked to be admitted with their cattle.

There has been much discussion about the site of the next station, *Etham*, which has always been considered as a city, and even as a fortress. The name Succoth, that of a region, shows that we are not to look for a *city* of Etham, but for a *district*, a *region* of that name. Saneha says in his papyrus that, leaving the Lake of Kemuer, he arrived with his companion at a place called *Atima*, which could not be very far distant. Let us now consult a document of the time of the Exodus, the papyrus Anastasi VI, and read in M. Brugsch's translation, "*We have allowed the tribes of the Shasu of the land of Atuma to pass the stronghold of King Menephtah of the land of Succoth, towards the lakes of Pithom of King Menephtah of the land of Succoth; in order to feed themselves and to feed their cattle in the great estate of Pharaoh.*" That is what I consider as the region of *Etham*, the land which the papyri call *Atima, Atma, Atuma*. It was inhabited by Shasu nomads, and as it was insufficient to nourish their cattle, they were obliged to ask to share the good pastures which had been assigned to the Israelites. The hieroglyphic determinative of its name indicates that it was a borderland. Both the nature of the land and its name seem to agree very well with what was said of Etham, that it was "on the edge of the wilderness" (*Exodus* XIII, 20).

Another reason which induces me to think that Etham was a *region*, and not a *city*, is that in *Numbers* (XXXIII, 6, 7, 8) we read of the "wilderness of Etham," in which the Israelites marched three

other, either by the name of the king who built them, or by some local circumstance; just as there are in Italy a considerable number of Torre. I should, therefore, with M. Ebers, place Migdol at the present station of the Serapeum. There the sea was not wide, and the water probably very shallow; there also the phenomenon which took place on such a large scale when the Israelites went through, must have been well known, as it is often seen now in other parts of Egypt. As at this point the sea was liable to be driven back under the influence of the east wind, and to leave a dry way, the Pharaohs were obliged to have there a fort, a *Migdol*, so as to guard that part of the sea, and to prevent the Asiatics of the desert from using this temporary gate to enter Egypt, to steal cattle and to plunder the fertile land which was round Pithom. That there was one spot particularly favourable for crossing because of this well-known effect of the wind, is indicated by the detailed description of the place where the Israelites are to camp. There is a striking difference between this description and the vague data which we find before and after. It is not only said that they are to camp near the sea, but the landmarks are given, Pi-Hahiroth, Migdol, Baal Zephon, so that they could not miss the spot, which, perhaps, was very restricted.

We have now the landmarks of the camping ground of the Israelites : on the north-west Pi-Hahiroth, Pikerehet, not very far from Pithom ; on the south-east Migdol, near the present Serapeum ; in front of them the sea; and opposite, on the Asiatic side, on some hill like Shekh Ennedek, Baal Zephon. There, in the space between the Serapeum and Lake Timsah, the sea was narrow, the water had not much depth, the east wind opened the sea, and the Israelites went through.

This seems to me, at present, the most probable route of the Exodus. I think it agrees best with what we know of the geographical names, and of the nature of the land. Besides, it does not suppose very long marches, which would have been quite impossible with a large multitude; the distances are not very great, and on that account the information which we owe to the Roman milestone is invaluable.

LIST OF EGYPTIAN GEOGRAPHICAL NAMES MENTIONED IN THE BIBLE, WITH REFERENCES.

BIBLE.	ANCIENT EGYPTIAN.	HEBREW.	SEPTUAGINT.	MODERN.	
ALEXANDRIA.—3 Macc.iii, 1. comp. Acts vi,9; xviii,24. AVEN.—Ez.xxx,17. (= On).	ÁNU.	†AVEN.	ALEXANDREIA. HELIOUPOLIS.	ALEXANDRIA. HELIOPOLIS, near Cairo.	Founded by Alexander the Great, B.C. 332.
BAAL ZEPHON.—Ex.xiv, 2, 9; Num.xxxiii,7.	?	BAAL TSEPHÓN, Baal of the North.	BEEL SEPPHON.	?	See 3rd ed. Naville's "Pithom," p. 31. M. Naville says that it must become hill opposite the Migdol of the Exodus, on the Asiatic side of the Red Sea.
BETH SHEMESH.—Jer. xliii,13. (= On).	ÁNU.—Its religious name was PER-RÁ (Pr-Rá) the abode or city of Ra, the sun-god; the great ascendal centre of his worship.	BETH SHEMESH, House of the Sun.	HELIOPOLIS EN ON. City of the Sun in On.	HELIOPOLIS, near Cairo.	The Ethiopia of the Greek and Roman geographers.
CUSH (the country).—Gen. ii, 13; x, 6, 7, 8; 1 Chron. i, 8, 9, 10.	KASH.—Denoted the districts south of the 1st cataract.	KUSH.	KHOUS.	NUBIA.	
EGYPT, river, stream of.—Num.xxxiv, 5; Josh.xv, 4; xv,47; 1 K. viii,65; 2 K. xxiv,7; Is.xxvii,12.	ÁTER ÁA, the great river (i.e. the Nile).	NEHAR MITSRAÍM, NAKHAL MITS-RAÍM, River of Mitsraim (Egypt).	POTAMOS AIGUPTOU, river of Egypt. KHEIMARROUS AIG-UPTOU, winterstream (or flood stream) of Egypt. PHARANX AIGUPTOU, (bed of a flood stream) of Egypt.	THE NILE, THE WÂDY EL 'ARÎSH.	The city of Rhinocorura (El 'Arîsh) with its Wâdy formed the frontier of Egypt towards Syria.
ETHAM.—Ex. xiii, 20; Num.xxxiii, 6, 7. Wilderness of, Num. xxxiii, 8.	*ÁTUMA, ÁTHMA, ÁTMA, a desert region beginning at Lake Timsah, and extending west and south of it near the Arabian gulf. OBS, QESEM.—Its religious name was PER SEPTU (Pr Septu).	ÉTHÁM. MIDBAR ÉTHÁM, wilderness of Etham.	RHINOCOROURA. OTHOM. BOUTHA. EERMOS, wilderness.		See 3rd ed. Naville's "Pithom," p. 28, and pp. 13–14 of this Atlas.
GOSHEN, city of.—Gen. xlvi, 28, 29.	The land which afterwards became the Arabian or Heroöpolitan Nome; the country about the city of Qeeem, without definite boundaries when occupied by the Israelites.	ERETS GOSHEN, land of Goshen.	GESEM, GEBEM GESEM ARABIAS (Geeem of Arabia). HEROONPOLIS (EN GE RAMESSE), Heroon-polis (in the land of Ramesee). GE GESEM ARABIAS, land of Geeem Arabia. GE GESEM, Land of Geeem.	SAFT EL HEN-NA, near Za-gazig. District around SAFT EL HEN-NA.	See Naville's "Goshen, and the Shrine of Saft el Henneh," and pp. 10—11 of this Atlas. Ditto ditto. Heroonpolis is really Pithom, and the Septuagint is here, as often, in error.
GOSHEN, land of.—Gen. xlv, 10; xlvi, 28, 34; xlvii, 1, 4, 6. [See RAMESES, land of].					

* Opinion is much divided on the subject of the reading and identification of these names: according to some, the name Edom is to be seen in them. Etham has also been identified with a fortress, "Khetem" in Egyptian; (see W. Max Müller, Asien und Europa, p. 185, and Sayce, The Higher Criticism and the Monuments, pp. 251-252, 261-262.

† The same Hebrew character as in the name ÓN, but differently pointed.

LIST OF EGYPTIAN GEOGRAPHICAL NAMES MENTIONED IN THE BIBLE.—(continued).

WITH REFERENCES.

BIBLE.	ANCIENT EGYPTIAN.	HEBREW.	SEPTUAGINT.	MODERN.	
Ham, land of.—Ps.lxxviii, 51; cv, 23; cvi, 22.	Kemt.—*The black land* (as distinguished from *the red land*, or desert).	Kham.	Kham.	Egypt.	
Hanes.—Is. xxx, 4.		Khanes.	Tafne.		*Tanis* in the Septuagint is of course an error. See, however, pp. 3–4 of Naville's *"Ahnas."*
Memphis (= Noph).—Hos. ix, 6.	Men-nefer, *the good or beautiful place.*	Moph.	Memphis.	Memphis, near Cairo.	The ancient capital of Egypt under the Old Kingdom or Empire.
Migdol.—(1) Ex.xiv, 2; Num. xxxiii, 7; (2) Jer. xliv, 1; xlvi, 14; and Ez. xxix, 10; xxx, 6, in margin R.V.	Makther.—A word of Semitic origin, signifying a fort, or tower.	Migdol, a watch-tower.	Magdolom.	(1) .... (2) Tell el Hêr. (?)	See 3rd ed. Naville's *"Pithom,"* p. 31, for (1), and pp. 15—16 of this, Atlas. (2) was on the frontier of Egypt.
Mizraim.—Gen. x, 6,	Compare the Egyptian division into the South and North countries.	Mitsraim, dual of Matsôr, a watch-tower. Used in the dual of the whole of Egypt; in the singular of the Delta only.	Mesraim.	Egypt (Upper and Lower).	Where the Hebrew gives Mitsraim, the English translation gives Egypt, except in this passage.
Naphtuhim (people of Memphis?).—Gen. x, 13; 1 Chron. i, 11.		Naphtukhim.	Nephthalim. Nephthalim.		
No (= No Amon).—Jer. xlvi, 25; Ez. xxx, 14,16,16; Nah. iii, 8 (A.V.)— No-Amon (= No).— Nah. iii, 8 (R.V.)	Net-Amen.—*The city of (the god) Amen.*	Nô, Nô Amôn.	Ammon. Diospolis.	Thebes.	The capital of Egypt under the Middle and New Kingdoms or Empires.
Noph.—Is. xix, 13; Jer. ii, 16; Ez. xxx, 13, 16.	Men-nefer, *the good or beautiful place.*	Noph.	Meris Ammon, the portion of Amen. Memphis.	Memphis, near Cairo.	The ancient capital of Egypt under the Old Kingdom or Empire.
On (see Aven and Beth Shemesh).—Gen. xli, 45, 50; xlvi, 20.	Anu.	Ôn.	Helioupolis.	Heliopolis, near Cairo.	
Pathros.—Is. xi, 11; Jer. xliv, 1; Ez. xxix, 14; xxx, 14.	Pa-ta-res, "*the South land.*"	Pathrôs.	Babulonia. Pathoures. Ge Pathoures.	Upper Egypt.	The Septuagint version, with Babylonia, shows a different reading.
Pathrusim (people of Pathros).—Gen. x, 14; 1 Chron. i, 12.		Pathrusim.	Pathrosmeim.		
Pibeseth.—Ez. xxx, 17.	Per Bast (Pi Bast) "*the Abode, or city of Bast,*" the cat-headed goddess.	Pibeseth.	Boubastos.	Tell Basta, near Zagazig.	See Naville's "*Bubastis.*"

LIST OF EGYPTIAN GEOGRAPHICAL NAMES MENTIONED IN THE BIBLE.—(continued).

WITH REFERENCES.

BIBLE.	ANCIENT EGYPTIAN.	HEBREW.	SEPTUAGINT.	MODERN.	
PIHAHIROTH.—Ex. xiv, 2, 9; Num. xxxiii, 7, 8; R.V. HAHIROTH.	*PEHOREHRET (PIQEREHRT).	PIHAHIROTH, the mouth of?	EPAULIS, farmstead; STOMA EIROTH, mouth of eiroth; EIROTH.	Ruins at the foot of Gebel Mariam.	See Naville's "Pithom" for his identification of Pihahiroth, p. 30.
PITHOM.—Ex. i, 11.	PER TUM (PI TUM), "the Abode, or city of Tum," god of the setting Sun.	PITHOM.	PEITHO.	TELL EL MASKHÛTEH, 12 miles from Ismailiah, near the railway station, Rameses.	See Naville's "Pithom," and p. 7 of this Atlas.
RAMESES, RAAMSES (city).—Ex. i, 11; xii, 37; Num. xxxiii, 3, 5. comp. Judith, i, 9.	QESEM?	RA'MESÊS.	RAMESSE.	SAFT EL HENNEH? [NEH?]	See Naville's "Goshen," p. 7. The identification is very uncertain.
RAMESES, land of.—Gen. xlvii, 11. See Septuagint reading of Gen. xlvi, 28, under GOSHEN, land of.	An area including the district of QESEM (Goshen).	ERETS RA'MESÊS, the land Raamses.	GE RAMESSE, the land of Ramesse.	Province of Sharkieh.	See 3rd ed. Naville's "Pithom," and p. 11 of this Atlas.
SEVENEH, R.V. (SYENE A.V.)—Ez. xxix, 10; xxx, 6. SHIHOR OF EGYPT, SIHOR.—1 Chron. xiii, 5; Josh. xiii, 3; Jer. ii, 18.		SEVENÊH. SHIKHÔR MITSRÂIM, SHIKHÔR of Egypt. SHIKHÔR.	SYENE. HOBIA AIGYPTOU, the frontier of Egypt.	ASWÂN. THE WÂDY EL 'ARÎSH.	At the Southern extremity of Egypt.
SHUR.—Gen. xvi, 7; xx, 1; xxv, 18; 1 Sam. xv, 7; xxvii, 8. (=wilderness of Etham), Ex. xv, 22. SIN.—Ez. xxx, 15, 16.		SHÛR. SÎN.	AOIKETOS, the uninhabited land. SOUR, GELAMPSOUR. SAIS, SYENE.	ET TÎNEH (?), PELUSIUM (?).	Septuagint apparently wrong.
SUCCOTH.—Ex. xii, 37; xiii, 20; Num. xxxiii, 5, 6.	THUKU or THUKET, a district containing Pithom.	SUKKÔTH.	SOKKHOTH.	District round TELL EL MASKHÛTEH.	See 3rd edition Naville's "Pithom," pp. 6, 7, 28, and p. 14 of this Atlas.
TAHPANHES, TAHAPANHES, TEHAPHNEHES.—Jer. ii, 16; xliii, 7, 8, 9; xliv, 1; xlvi, 14; Ez. xxx, 18. comp. Judith, i, 9. (comp. Hanes).		TAKHPANKHÊS, TAKHPENÊS. TEKHAPHNEHÊS.	TAPHNAI.	DEFENEH, about 10 miles S.E. of Tanis, San.	Daphnae was a settlement of Greek mercenaries and traders, founded about B.C. 680 by Psammetichus I, of the xxvith Dynasty.
ZOAN.—Num. xiii, 22; Ps. lxxviii, 12, 43; Is. xix, 11, 13; xxx, 4; Ez. xxx, 14.	ZAN.	ZO'AN.	TANIS.	SÂN, near Lake Menzaleh, — reached by rail and boat from Zagazig.	See Petrie's "Nebesheh, and Defenneh," issued with "Tanis ii." See Petrie's "Tanis i," and "Tanis ii."

* This identification is not altogether accepted, partly on philological grounds; but the place must have been in the land of Thuku or its immediate vicinity.

CHRONOLOGICAL
TABLE OF THE EGYPTIAN DYNASTIES.

N.B.—The dates in the following table as far as the xixth Dynasty are those which Professor Petrie has given in his Lectures as approximative. The uncertainty for the early period is very great, but the date assigned to the xviiith Dynasty is believed to be correct within one century. The later dates are taken chiefly from Böckh and Wiedemann ; from the xxvith Dynasty to the end of the native rule the error cannot be more than a few years.

OLD KINGDOM OR EMPIRE.

DYNASTY.			CAPITAL.		DATES B.C.
I	Thinite	... ...	This, near Abydos	...	... 4782
II	Thinite	... ...	This		... 4519
III	Memphite	... ...	Memphis, near Cairo	...	... 4217
IV	Memphite	... ...	Memphis	...	... 4003
V	Memphite	... ...	Memphis	...	... 3726
VI	Elephantine	...	Elephantine, near Syene		... 3508
VII	Memphite	... ...	Memphis	...	... 3327
VIII	Memphite	... ...	Memphis	...	... 3257
IX	Heracleopolite	...	Ahnas (Heracleopolis Magna)	...	3111
X	Heracleopolite	...	Ahnas „ „		... 3011
XI	Theban, or Diospolite		Thebes (Diospolis)	...	... 2826

MIDDLE KINGDOM OR EMPIRE.

XII	Theban, or Diospolite		Thebes (Diospolis)	...	... 2783
XIII	Theban „ „		Thebes „	...	... 2570
· XIV	Xoite	... ...	Xoïs, in the Delta	...	... 2117

(HYKSOS PERIOD).

XV	Hyksôs	... ...	Avaris (Tanis ?)	...	... 2003
XVI	Hyksôs	... ...	Avaris „	...	... 1933

NEW KINGDOM OR EMPIRE.

XVII	Theban, or Diospolite		Thebes (Diospolis)	...	... 1743
XVIII	Theban „ „		Thebes „	...	... 1592
XIX	Theban „ „		Thebes „	...	... 1327
XX	Theban „ „		Thebes „	...	... 1183
XXI	Tanite,and the Priest Kings		Tanis and Thebes	...	... 1048
XXII	Bubastite	... ...	Bubastis	...	... 934
XXIII	Tanite	... ...	Tanis	...	... 814
XXIV	Saïte ...	... ...	Saïs	...	... 725
XXV	Ethiopian	... ...	Thebes	...	... 719
XXVI	Saïte ...	... ...	Saïs	...	... 665

PERSIAN PERIOD.	LAST NATIVE DYNASTIES.
XXVIIth Dynasty [Susa] B.C. 527	XXVIII Saïte ... Saïs B.C. 408
	XXIX Mendesian Mendes 387
	XXX Sebennyte Sebennytus 350

MACEDONIAN RULE.—B.C. 332—B.C. 305.

PTOLEMAIC PERIOD.—B.C. 305—B.C. 30.

ROMAN PERIOD.—B.C. 30—A.D. 394.

BYZANTINE RULE.—A.D. 394—A.D. 638.

A.D. 638, THE ARAB CONQUEST.

PRINCIPAL AUTHORITIES
ON THE GEOGRAPHY AND HISTORY OF ANCIENT EGYPT.

I.—CLASSICAL WRITERS.

HERODOTUS (B.C. 484–400 [?]).—Book II, and part of Book III of his History are devoted to Egypt, where he had travelled, note-book in hand, about 450 B.C., during the reign of the Persian Artaxerxes.

MANETHO (time of Ptolemy II, Philadelphus, third century B.C.)—He was an Egyptian priest, with temple archives at his command, but wrote in Greek, the language of the court. It is only from his History of Egypt that we have any literary record of the dates and succession of the dynasties, and of that History only such fragments survive as were incorporated in the writings of Josephus, and the Christian chroniclers; it was written soon after B.C. 271.

ERATOSTHENES (B.C. 276–196).—A fragment of his "Chronographia," preserved by Syncellus, contains a list of thirty-eight Theban Kings.

DIODORUS SICULUS (contemporary of Julius Caesar and Augustus).— Book I of his "Historical Library" is exclusively devoted to Egypt, and later portions of his work give us invaluable information relating to the Persian period. He travelled in Egypt about B.C. 57.

STRABO (about B.C. 54–A.D. 20: Augustus to Tiberius).—His "Geography" takes into account all that he found to be most interesting and characteristic in every country. Book XVII deals with Egypt, where he travelled B.C. 24.

PLINY, the Elder (A.D. 23–79).—His "Natural History," which he compiled from literary sources, and not from observation, incidentally describes some of the products and monuments of Egypt, often as marvels, and summarises the geography.

JOSEPHUS, Flavius (A.D. 37 to about 100).—In his Greek "Jewish Antiquities," Josephus gives a fuller account of the Egyptian life of the Children of Israel than that given in the Old Testament. In his treatise defending Jewish culture and antiquity against the attack of Apion, he quotes many ancient authors in reference to the Exodus; above all, he gives long extracts from Manetho's history of Egypt.

PLUTARCH (about A.D. 50—130).—There are references to Egypt in his "Parallel Lives," and other works; his treatise on Isis and Osiris is exclusively devoted to considering the Egyptian religion.

PTOLEMY, the Geographer (flourished in Alexandria A.D. 139–160, surviving Antoninus Pius).—He describes Africa and Egypt in Book IV of his "Geography" of the then known world. This work was the great geographical text-book of Europe for more than a thousand years.

ANTONINI ITINERARIUM (made by successive Emperors down to the Antonines).—This is the official Itinerary of the whole Roman empire of the period, in which the principal and cross-roads, together with a list of the places and stations upon them, and the distances from one place to another, in Roman miles, are all given.

AFRICANUS (wrote in 221 A.D.)—He composed a Chronicle of the History of the World. As regards Egypt, his history was largely based on that of Manetho. His work is lost, with the exception of certain extracts preserved by other writers.

EUSEBIUS (A.D. 264—340).—Allusions to Egypt are contained in various writings of Eusebius. His chronicle of Egyptian history is chiefly taken from the lost work of Africanus, and is most fully preserved in an Armenian translation.

GEORGIUS SYNCELLUS (lived in the 8th Century A.D.)—This chronicler also made large extracts from the writings of his predecessors, including those of Africanus, and hence of Manetho.

II.—Modern Works.

Brown, Major.—*Lake Moeris and the Fayûm.*

Brugsch, H.—*Dictionnaire Géographique. Geographische Inschriften.*
* *Geschichte Ægyptens unter den Pharaonen.*

Catalogue des Monuments et Inscriptions de l'Égypte Antique. Div. I. Tome I. de la frontière de Nubie à Kom Ombos: par J. de Morgan, U. Bouriant, *etc.*

Dümichen, J., and Meyer, E.—*Geschichte des alten Aegyptens.*

Erman, A.—**Ægypten und Ægyptisches Leben im Altertum.*

Expeditions :—

Description de l'Égypte ou recueil des observations et des recherches qui ont été faites en Égypte pendant l'expédition de l'armée française. 10 vols. text ; 14 vols. plates.

Champoléion, J. F.—*Monuments de l'Egypte et de la Nubie.* 4 vols. of plates. *Notices descriptives.* 2 vols.

Rosellini, I.— *I Monumenti dell' Egitto e della Nubia.* 9 vols. text; 3 vols. plates.

Lepsius, R.—*Denkmäler aus Ægypten und Æthiopien.* 12 vols. plates; 1 vol. text.

Mémoires publiés par les membres de la Mission Archéologique française au Caire.

Journals:—

Zeitschrift für Ægyptische Sprache und Alterthumskunde.

Recueil de travaux relatifs à la philologie et à l'archéologie Égyptiennes et Assyriennes.

Revue Égyptologique.

Lepsius, R.—*Königsbuch.*

Mariette, A.—*Voyage dans la haute Égypte. Karnak. Abydos. Deir-el-Bahari. Dendérah.*

Maspero, G.—*Histoire ancienne des Peuples de l'Orient. Études de Mythologie et d'Archéologie Égyptiennes.* * *Histoire de l'Orient.*

Petrie, W. M. Flinders.—*Ten Years Digging in Egypt. Memoirs: A Season in Egypt, Hawara, Kahun, Illahun, Medum,* and *Tell el Amarna. History of Egypt* (forthcoming).

Societies:—

Excavations and Survey Memoirs of the Egypt Exploration Fund (see end of this Atlas).

Proceedings and *Transactions of the Society of Biblical Archaeology.*

Wiedemann, A.—*Ægyptische Geschichte.*

Wilkinson, Sir Gardner—*Manners and Customs of the Ancient Egyptians.*

* May be had in English translation.

GENERAL MAP OF ANCIENT EGYPT

WITH

ADJACENT COUNTRIES.

GENERAL MAP OF MODERN EGYPT
AND ADJACENT COUNTRIES.

MEDITERRANEAN SEA

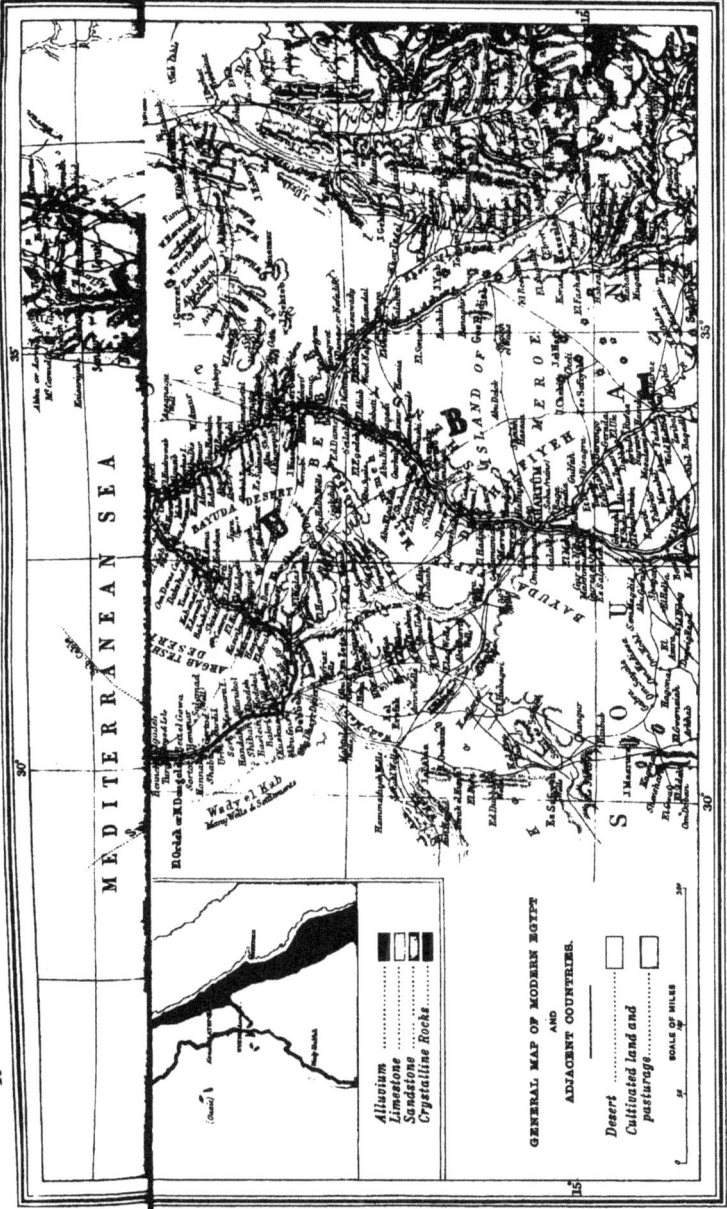

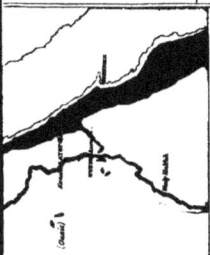

Alluvium
Limestone
Sandstone
Crystalline Rocks

GENERAL MAP OF MODERN EGYPT
AND
ADJACENT COUNTRIES.

Desert
Cultivated land and
pasturage.

SCALE OF MILES

TABLE OF THE NOMES, WITH THEIR CAPITALS AND THE GODS WORSHIPPED IN THEM (I to XX of Lower Egypt and XX to XXII of Upper Egypt).

	Nome.		Capital City.	Deity.
I.	Ȧnb-ḥez	White wall	Men-nefer	Ptaḥ
II.	Khẹnsu (?)		Sekhem	Hor-ur (Aroëris)
III.	Ȧment	West	Ȧmu	Hathor
IV.	Sap-qemȧ	Southern target	Zeqȧ	Sebek
V.	Sap-meḥ	Northern target	Sau	Neïth
VI.	Ka-khas (?)		Khasuu	Rȧ
VII.	Nefer(?)ȧmenti	East harpoon	Senti-nefer	Ȧmen-rȧ
VIII.	Nefer(?)ȧbti	West harpoon	Per-Tum	Tum
IX.	Ȧty	Liege lord	Per-Usar-neb-teṭ	Osiris
X.	Kȧ-kem	Black bull	Ḥet-Ta-ḥer-ȧb {	Horus-"Khenti-Khety"
XI.	Ka-ḥeseb		Per-mȧka	Set
XII.	Theb-ȧḥt (?)		Theb-neter	Ȧnḥer
XIII.	Heqa-ȧmes		Ȧnu	Tum
XIV.	Khent-ȧbt		Zaru	Horus
XV.	Tekh (?)	Ibis	Khemenu	Thoth
XVI.	Ḥa-mehyt (?)	Fish	Per-ba-neb-tat	Ba-en-ṭaṭ
XVII.	Sma-beḥtet		Pa-khen-en-Ȧmen	Ȧmen-rȧ
XVIII.	Ȧm-khent	Upper prince	Per-Bast	Bast
XIX.	Ȧm-peḥ	Lower prince	Ȧmt	Uazyt (Buto)
XX.	Septu-ḳemhes (?)		Qesem, Per-Sopṭ	Septu

(The last three Nomes of Upper Egypt contained in the Map of Lower Egypt.)

XX.	Ȧm-khent	Upper	Henen-seten	Her-she-ef
XXI.	Ȧm-peḥ	Lower	Smen-Hor	Khnem
XXII.	Matenu	Knife	Ṭep-ȧḥ (?)	Hathor

[*To face Map III.*]

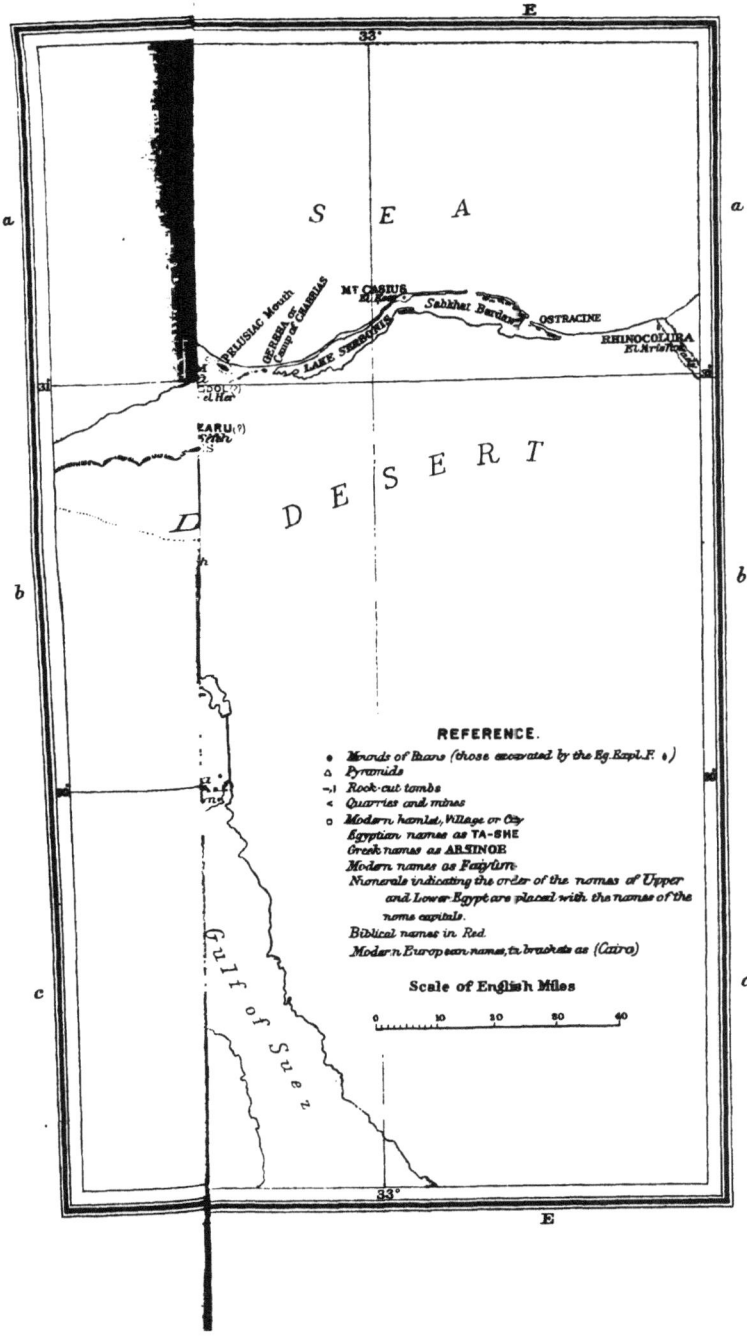

E

33°

a   a

S   E   A

M⸀ CASIUS
PELUSIAC Mouth
GENERA or
Camp of CHABRIAS
Sekkhet Bardawil
OSTRACINE
LAKE SERBONIS
RHINOCOLURA
El Arish
el Has

TARU(?)

D   E   S   E   R   T

D

b   b

Gulf of Suez

c   c

REFERENCE.

- ● Mounds of Ruins (those excavated by the Eg. Expl. F. ●)
- △ Pyramids
- ⌐,ı Rock-cut tombs
- ◄ Quarries and mines
- □ Modern hamlet, Village or City
  Egyptian names as TA-SHE
  Greek names as ARSINOE
  Modern names as Faiyûm
  Numerals indicating the order of the nomes of Upper
     and Lower Egypt are placed with the names of the
     nome capitals.
  Biblical names in Red.
  Modern European names, in brackets as (Cairo)

Scale of English Miles

0   10   20   30   40

33°

E

TABLE OF THE NOMES, WITH THEIR CAPITALS AND THE GODS WORSHIPPED IN THEM (IX to XIX of Upper Egypt).

	Nome.		Capital City.	Deity.
IX.		Men (?)	Åpu	Min
X.		Uazet	Green	Thebu	Hathor
XI.		Set	Set-animal	Shashotep	Khnem
XII.		Ṭu-f	Mount of the Cerastes (?)	Net-ent-bak	Horus
XIII.		Atef-khent	Upper Atef	Saut	Upuat
XIV.		Atef-peḥ	Lower Atef	·Qesi	Hathor
XV.		Unt	Hare	Khemnu	Thoth
XVI.		Maḥez	Oryx	Ḥebnu	Khnem
XVII.		Ȧnpu	Jackal	Kasa	Anubis
XVIII.		Sep		Ḥet-Benu, Sep	Anubis
XIX.		Uaseb (?)		Per-Màza	Set

[To face Map IV.]

BEN^I SUÊF TO EKHMÎM.

TABLE OF THE NOMES, WITH THEIR CAPITALS AND THE GODS WORSHIPPED IN THEM (I to IX of Upper Egypt).

		Nome.		Capital City.	Deity.
I.		Ta-khent (?)		Abu	Khnem
II.		Uthes-Ḥor	Hawk-perch	Ṭebu	Horus
III.		Ten (?)		Nekheb	Nekhebyt
IV.		Uas	Uas-sceptre	Ȧpt, Net	Amen
V.		Herui	Two hawks	Qebti	Min
VI.		Ȧat-ṭe (?)		Ta-n-terer	Hathor
VII.		Seshesht	Sistrum	Ḥet-seshesht, Ḥet	Hathor
VIII.		Abez	Reliquary	Teni	Ȧnḥer
IX.		Men (?)		Ȧpu	Min

[*To face Map V.*]

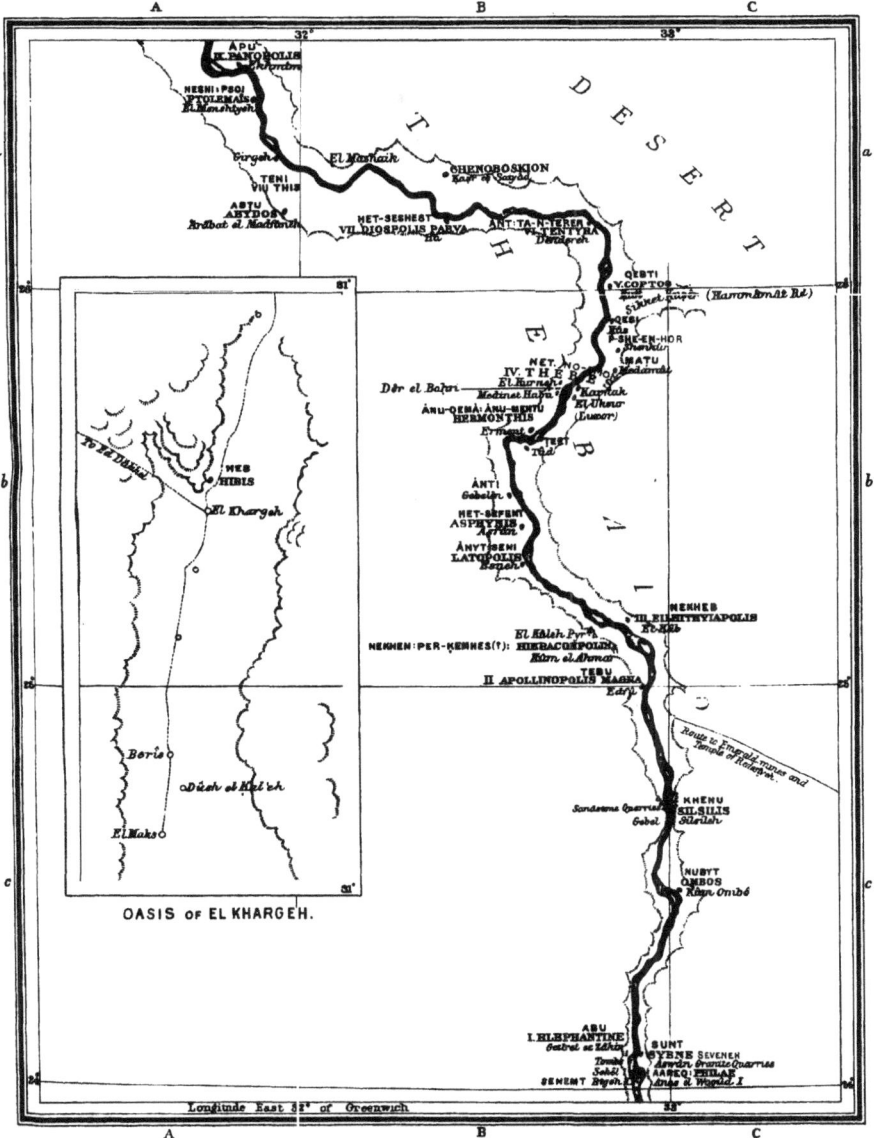

OASIS of EL KHARGEH.

EKHMÎM TO PHILAE.

A B C

31° 32° 33°

a *a*

1ᵗ Cataract
SEMNET: Dígeh
TA-HET
Debôd

Kertassi

TAPHIS
Taifa
TERMES, TALMIS
Kalabsheh

b *b*

Dendûr
PER-PTAH
TUTZIS
Gerf Husêyn

PSERKET
PSELCHIS
Dakkeh
Kortih

DODECA-SCHOENUS

SEK
CONTRA-PSELCHIS
Kubbân

Ofedtneh
Maharrakeh
KEMSA
TACOMPSO I.

Es Sebû'a

Amâdeh

Der
MÂM
PREMIS
Ibrîm

DESERT

Abu Simbel
'Addeh
Beyêg

Faras
Aksheh

DESERT

SEMEH
BOON
Wady Halfeh
2ⁿᵈ Cataract

c *c*

d *d*

31° Longitude East of Greenwich. 32° 33°

A B C

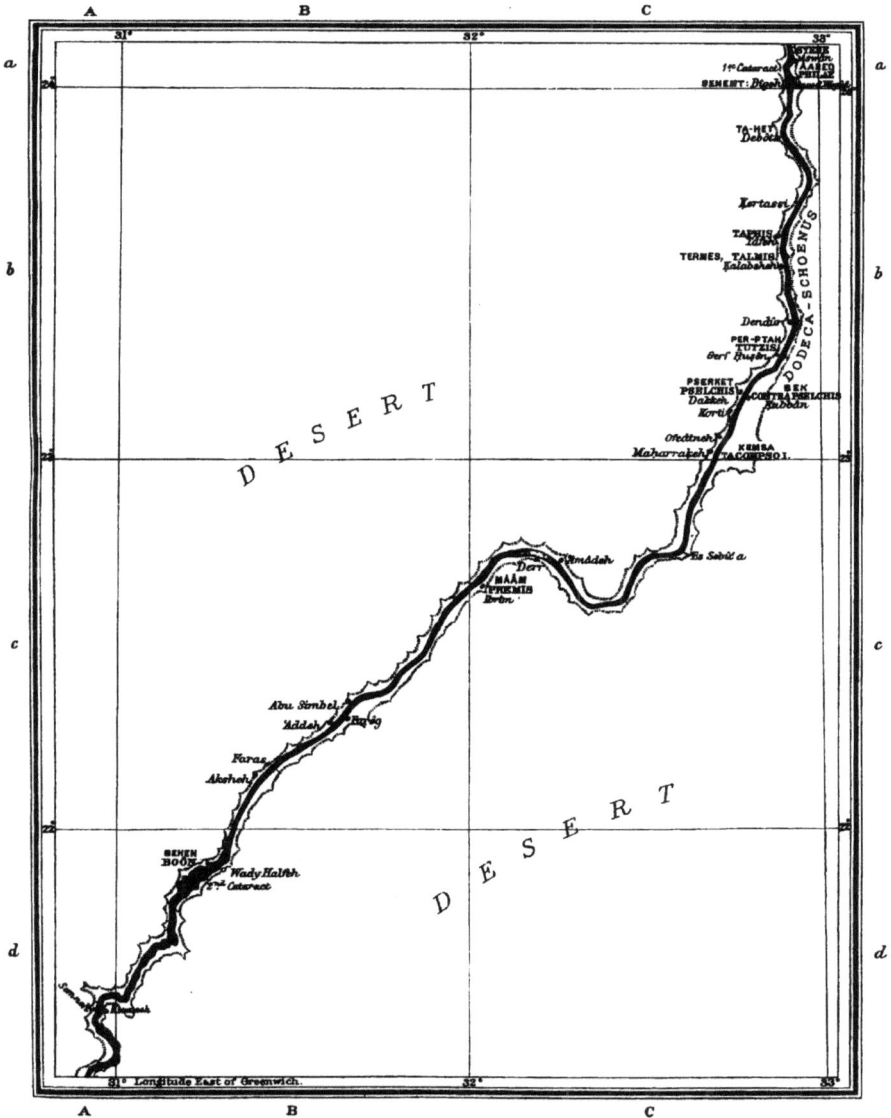

ASWÂN TO SEMNEH.

A   B   C   D   E

30°   31°   32°   33°   34°

Semneh *Kummeh*

a

21

b

20

Soleb

c

3ᵈ Cataract
Tombos Iᵈ
Argó Iᵈ

19

Ruins

D E S E R T

Ruins

d

4ᵗʰ Cataract
TU UÁS
Gebel Barkal
NAPET
NAPATA
El Kurneh
Nuri
Bankaasi
Ruins

5ᵗʰ Cataract

18

Berber
ASTABORAS *Atbara*

e

D E S E R T

17

Ruins
Ruins
BAKRAUA
MEROË
Begerawieh

f

Ruins
6ᵗʰ Cataract
Wady es Softa
Náka

Scale of English Miles
25   30   100

16

g

0 5 10

Kharṭûm
Soba

31° Long. East of Greenwich.   32°   33°   34°

A   B   C   D   E

SEMNEH TO KHARṬÛM.

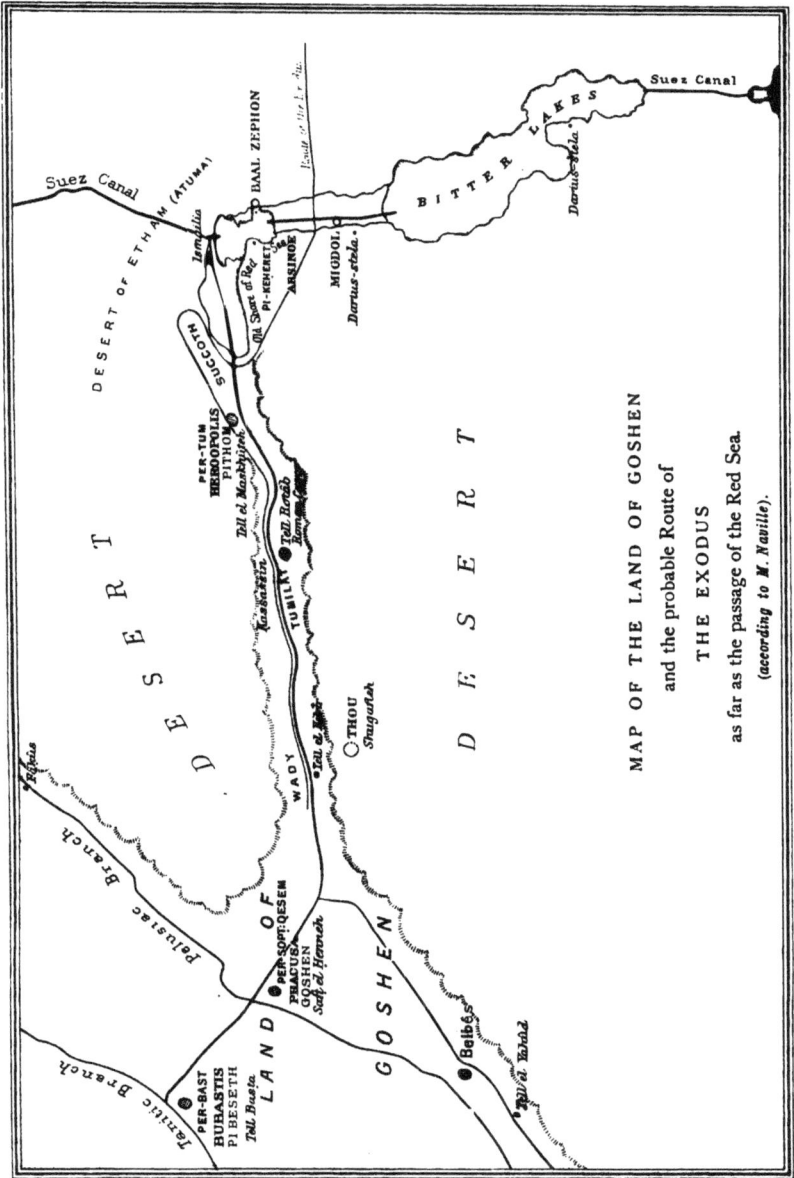

MAP OF THE LAND OF GOSHEN
and the probable Route of
THE EXODUS
as far as the passage of the Red Sea.
(according to M. Naville).

INDEX TO MAPS OF ANCIENT EGYPT, ETHIOPIA, &c.

Nos. I. & III.—VIII.

INDEX TO MAPS OF ANCIENT EGYPT, ETHIOPIA, ETC.